dentsu online REPUTATION management handbook

Popular Prakashan
www.popularprakashan.com

AIRCEL academy

Popular Prakashan Pvt. Ltd.
301, Mahalaxmi Chambers
22, Bhulabhai Desai Road
Mumbai 400026

ISBN : 978-81-7991-654-4
(4402)

Disclaimer:
Dentsu Marcom India Pvt Ltd and the publishers make no representations or warranties with respect to any information contained in this book and shall not be responsible or liable for any errors, inaccuracies or omissions in relation to the information contained herein. We acknowledge and thank all the sources on the worldwide web that we have drawn upon for the information in this book. However, neither the publishers nor Dentsu Marcom India Ltd take responsibility for the same.

Printed by
Tara Art Printers Pvt. Ltd.
B-4, Hans Bhawan, B.S.Z. Marg,
New Delhi - 110002

Published by
Harsha Bhatkal for
Popular Prakashan Pvt. Ltd.
301, Mahalaxmi Chambers
22, Bhulabhai Desai Road
Mumbai 400026

AIRCEL academy

This book is the combined effort of

DilipKarthik J

Parul Rangnekar Singh

Sourav Dutta

Ritesh Sharma

Snigdha Nandan

Stuti Shalini Guria

Girish Sharma

S.M.Salim

Naresh Gupta

Sudheer Varanasi

Suraj Nagappa

Gaurav Tandon

Special Thanks to

Rahul Saighal

Basant Dhawan

Himanshu Sharma

Rajesh Aggarwal

Krishna Prasad

And all others in Dentsu and Aircel who were directly or indirectly involved in the creation of the book

Foreword

Washington Post Staff Writers, Susan Kinzie and Ellen Nakashima, wrote a front-page article, "Calling in Pros to Redefine Your Google Image", in The Washington Post on Monday, July 2, 2007.

As I write this Preface to this Dentsu ORM Handbook, the opening part of their article seems a great intro to this subject (though it is 3 years+ since they wrote the piece), and this book. Allow me to quote,

"At the height of the cyber-abuse, Sue Scheff, a consultant to parents of troubled teens, would type her name in a Google search box and brace herself: Up would pop page after page of attack postings.

Sue Scheff is destroying lives. She is a con. She takes kickbacks. She is the biggest fraud there ever was.

The stream of negative comments began in 2002 after a woman who had sought advice from Scheff turned on her. The postings appeared on PTA Web sites in Florida, where Scheff lives. On bulletin boards and online forums. There were even YouTube videos threatening her.

She sued for defamation and won an $11.3 million verdict, but the attacks only got worse. In December, Scheff turned to ReputationDefender, a year-old firm that promised to help her cleanse her virtual reputation. She no longer dreads a Google search on her name. Most of the links on the all-important first page are to her own Web site and a half-dozen others created by ReputationDefender to promote her work on teen pregnancy and teen depression.

"They created Sue-Scheff.net," she said. "They created SueScheff.net. They created SueScheff.org. . . . They created my MySpace account, for God's sake. I didn't know how to do any of this stuff."

Google's ubiquity as a research tool has given rise to a new industry: online identity management. The proliferation of blogs and Web sites can allow angry clients, jealous lovers or ruthless competitors to define a person's identity. Whether true or not, their words can have far-reaching effects ..."

Anyone of us could well be in the shoes of Sue Scheff.

Wikipedia defines Reputation Management as the process of tracking an entity's actions and other entities' opinions about those actions; reporting on those actions and opinions; and reacting to that report creating a feedback loop. As more and more of us Google to know more about competitors, clients, associates and friends, Online Reputation Management is becoming critical in our everyday life : as a corporation, as a community, as an individual. This is more so since the good and the bad remain permanently in cyber-space smearing or enhancing reputations.

The Dentsu ORM Handbook, after the stupendous success of our Social Media Handbook, is yet another attempt by Team Dentsu to simplify and demystify a topic that is today robust and relevant

Sandeep Goyal

Preface

In the same Washington Post article that Sandeep Goyal refers to in his Preface, there is a very interesting section on Dodging Mudballs.E-mails from friends started showing up three years ago in a Washington lobbyist's in-basket: Have you seen this?

Over decades in the capital, she had developed a thick skin. But after she took on a foreign regime as a client, an online magazine bashed her. The story was factual, but the tone nasty. Then a blogger wrote that she slept with someone to get a big contract. A political blog posted an e-mail she had written about secret campaign strategy. Truth mixed with rumor. Rumor mixed with lies.

Like Scheff (in Sandeep's Preface), she realized that the items that made her cringe came up high on the Google results page and stayed there, month after month. Her firm depended on her reputation. The lobbyist would speak only on condition of anonymity because she did not want the attacks to resume.

"There's no policing, no rules, no standards," she said. Bloggers are "cowboys," she said. "It's the wild, wild West."

Then one day she heard a talk by Nino Kader, an ORM specialist. His new company, he said, could reshape a person's online image.

She signed up.

Kader started with a printout of the top 100 hits on a Google search and went through them one by one, asking whether individual results -- such as her campaign contributions -- were good, bad or neutral.

He asked what she wanted the world to know about her. Then he started digging for good things, like an op-ed piece she had written and television interviews she had given that he could post on YouTube. He pitched stories about her to various publications. And he created links from popular sites to those online stories to entice the search engine.

Now her firm's Web site is the first result and other good ones follow.

Still, a story she hates remains on the first page.

"I'm in the early stages," she said. "I've already seen progress."

Companies today need to outthink Google. Search engines comb the Web with complex and ever-shifting algorithms, evaluating relevance and authority by looking at many factors. The corporation needs to stay ahead in this game. This can be pro-active (hence well planned and well executed) or it can be reactive (hence perhaps tackled in a more knee-jerk manner). But there is no evading the reality of Online Reputation Management.

We at Aircel, more specifically the Aircel Academy, are proud to once again associate with Team Dentsu in creating this Handbook ... the previous attempt with Social Media has become a bestseller. I hope this book too is enlightening to readers and a handy reference book for seasoned practitioners.

Gurdeep Singh

Aircel Academy

Our people are our greatest resources – they are ones who make Aircel what it is today. And Sustained growth can only be achieved when our people are nurtured.

That is the reason why the Aircel Academy came into being. To maximize the growth potential of every Aircelite. To ensure a holistic growth, encompassing both individual development and enhanced contribution to the organization. To create the future leaders who will look to the future, and not the past. And master a process of continually creating new solutions to meet ever changing challenges.

The Aircel Academy, located in the business hub of Gurgaon, is a sprawling 25,000 square feet campus, equipped with state of the art learning tools. Inviting the best teachers from within and without the organization, it will bring you the best training in the field of technology, sales, service management, professional support services and general management.

With cutting edge virtual classrooms and offsite training modules, the Aircel Academy is designed to reach every single Aircelite, no matter where you are located.

Come, explore the Aircel Academy. Let us grow together and take Aircel to a new high.

Table of Contents

FOREWORD IV

PREFACE VI

CHAPTER-1 : INTRODUCTION 1

CHAPTER-2 : HOW AND WHERE? 7

CHAPTER-3 : BUILDING ONLINE PRESENCE 17

CHAPTER-4 : TOOLS AND CODES 41

CHAPTER-5 : CASE STUDIES 63

CHAPTER-6 : GLOSSARY 73

CONCLUSION 81

BIBLIOGRAPHY 82

Introduction

1

Why ORM?

Why should you as a company care about online reputation management? Isn't that out of your control? In the real world, yes. Online, your reputation has a much larger audience- anyone who wants to, can bring up a list of results about you.

Who's writing about you? It's not just the digital avatars of journalists but your consumers. With the increase in the number of online communication channels, people are talking about every aspect of their life online.

This includes you and your effect on your consumers' lives. Earlier, these conversations would happen in real time, around the water cooler. Now, they occur simultaneously, on the water cooler that is the net, and are documented in perpetuity. More people are talking, more and more people are listening.

How then, can you influence your online reputation? Well please read on to explore and understand the nuances of online reputation management.

Reputation is critical. Reputation means how positively, or negatively, a company or similar institution is perceived by its key stakeholders. The success of any organization or entity depends on the people or entities that the company or institution relies on. The image they have of an organization would hence directly affect the success of the entity. For many for-profit companies, typical stakeholders might include customers, employees, suppliers, or financial analysts. For governments or political entities such as Congress, BJP stakeholders are, above all, the electorate.

Who should care about ORM?

In the pre Internet era, reputation was easier to control. Companies doled out information on their activities to the media, which informed consumers. Today's online world has decentralized and democratized this reputation creation. Citizen journalism has resulted in consumers participating in shaping your reputation. Hence, corporate cannot push the perception they want consumers to have online; they must recognize that they are one of the participants, along with their consumers in the creation of the company's reputation.

The reputations of an organization, its brands and employees are inter-related. The country of origin can affect an organization's reputation. Another influence on a company's reputation is the industry it belongs to. Competition also affects a company's reputation. If one company's reputation slides, the others look better in comparison. The reputation of the top management, like the CEO's reputation also affects the reputation of the organization. Small individually, but significant when taken together, are the ways in which each employee can influence over the company's reputation within his or her circle of friends, customers and family. Take advantage of the nature of the internet as a medium. Listen to customer feedback and what they need online. Design your products according to their requirements. Sit back and watch the positive feedback come in.

Even as an individual, you need to be careful about what your online persona is saying about you. Today, it is much easier for anyone with access to the Internet to find out, with the click of a mouse, about your past and present. What if a negative comment has been left on your blog? Learn how to manage your personal brand by highlighting your achievements on the right sites so that they are search friendly. You should also be aware of how you can minimize the impact of negative news about you by ensuring that positive content about you shows up first on search engines.

What is ORM?

When you monitor search engine result pages and any mentions in online media about your brand, company name, service or product, you are engaging in online reputation management.

Few companies do that on an ongoing basis. However, with the growth in consumer generated media, companies need to reorient themselves to the change in the online landscape.

Now that there is much more information about any particular brand, company, service or product available on the web, it is important that people searching for information on your company or brand see positive information first. Even if there is no information available on you online, that is a problem. It shows people don't care enough about your company to be talking about it.

For instance, Ebay was one of the first companies to use feedback from user generated content. Consumers gave ratings on other users of Ebay based on their interaction with them as buyers or sellers. Hence buyers and sellers were given reputations which helped other users decide whether they wanted to transact with them.

Traditional PR vs ORM

There are major, fundamental differences in how traditional media and ORM serve up news and information. The public also consumes, evaluates and remembers information they see in search engines differently from what they see in print.

Traditional PR is temporary

Traditional media is cyclical. News is refreshed each day. Bad publicity lasts only as long as the paper is on the newsstand, and after that it lingers faintly in most people's memories. That negative memory can be effectively offset by putting a "positive spin" on things.

Online information is permanent

Search engines index information "permanently." As long as a page is live on a webserver somewhere – the search engine will probably keep "listing" it somewhere in the search results. It will usually remain in the index until the website goes out of business. Even if you manage to get some "positive buzz" right on the front page, the negative information will probably still be there – right in their faces.

Search Engines directly invite scrutiny and comparison

Search engines naturally encourage people to compare a variety of contrasting web pages, side by side. There's a ton of junk on the web, and people have become very discerning about the credibility of content they're consuming. Many people can spot fake reviews and PR puffery a mile away.

CSR and ORM

Although actions speak louder than words, you must make yourself heard if you are doing well. Participating in community projects can lessen the negative fallout in case the company's reputation is at stake. Reputation is an intangible asset that accounts for +- 10% of a company's market value. Corporate social responsibility is a major component of a company's reputation. More peer to peer recommendations tend to happen if the company is active in social service. Recruiting employees and retaining them is also easier in this case. As you need to ensure that top search results are positive, highlight your CSR activities for the same. Maximum benefit accrues when your CSR activities are aligned with the industry you are in. However, highlighting your CSR activities during a crisis may make your viewers cynical. It is far better to participate in CSR activities and communicate this on a continuous basis.

How and Where?

2

In the introduction we have understood the importance of ORM and its potential. It is important that we understand how we utilize ORM and where we should apply ORM. The basic of ORM is the fact your online activities define your reputation. There are basic steps to start with and key points to consider for ORM. Read on to understand all these parameters and learn to monitor your reputation online.

Your online activities: you are what you do

Influence reputation engines by doing good work and providing better after sales service. Solicit recommendations. Potential customers who see a large number of fairly positive ratings are likely to be more disposed to you than great ratings from a few people.

Reputation engines track user reviews on other users in a business context. Consumers to consumer marketplaces rely on them to bridge the disparity between the buyer and the seller. The seller is at an advantage as the buyer only sees the goods after paying, online in an offline transaction. In case buyers are unhappy, they can give poor ratings to the seller and influence his reputation as perceived by later potential buyers. Address customer concerns in feedback and link to positive reviews on your website. Become a highly rated reviewer. Try reading books in your area of expertise and then reviewing them on sites like Amazon.com. You could also write reviews on many items at sites like mouthshut.com.

Starting points of ORM

For starters, you can communicate more online. Share your knowledge, your expertise on the industry you belong to. You can positively influence your reputation in this manner.

A favourable reputation is coveted- but difficult to possess. It is built over time, and is the result of others' perception of your company's work and trustworthiness. A good reputation serves as a shortcut for consumers when they are deciding which company to choose. Even if they have not personally experienced your company's brands, your company's reputation serves as a barometer to indicate what other consumers think of your brand.

While you may be adding content to your company website, a dissatisfied consumer may be writing a scathing blog post about your brand. The dynamic nature of online conversations, with others joining the juggernaut, makes it imperative that you be aware of these conversations before they get out of hand.

ORM Methodology

The three steps involved in Online Reputation Management are:

1. Monitor

Monitor and track what is being said online

You want to know what is being said about your brand. You should be aware that ordinary people influence how the general public views your brand. It is very easy for anyone to publish information on CGM sites such as blogs, podcasts, and opinion forums. You must monitor these online conversations.

However, the size and complexity of the internet, coupled with the speed at which news travels, means that it is difficult to continuously monitor all that is being said.

To address this problem, you need an early warning system to alert you of all news relating to your brand, so you may remedy when the situation needed. There are internet monitoring services available that do the work for you. Such monitoring systems not only inform you of news and information relating to your brand, but will also help you to gather market intelligence and assess developing trends.

Once a monitoring system is in place for your brand you should also track other information such as competing brands and organizations, industry terms, as well as general industry news.Monitoring gives you immediate heads-up if adverse information is appearing.

2. Analyze

Analyze how the visible information affects your brand, your reputation

Your search engine space is dynamic and constantly changing as new sites are added to the mix and as search engines alter their algorithms. You need to develop an understanding of your search engine environment and of your competition.

First of all, undertake an analysis of your search engine space. Look at the sites listed in search results for your brand. List the sites that offer positive information and those that are negative. Determine what types of sites they are - blog, forum, consumer review, etc. Assign a value to their quality – page rank, number of links, influence, etc. Determine which results you may want to move up or down the list. This will help you understand the scale of the work involved.

3. Influence

Influence the results by participating in the conversation and eliminating negative sites

Influence online conversations by being actively involved in them. Your participation will give you the opportunity to improve the perception of your brand. Take an active part in your industry conversation by becoming a regular contributor to blogs and forums within your industry. Lead the conversation about your brand.

First steps

Evaluate the About Us section of your company website. Is it communicating the image you want to showcase? Are you building a positive image in the signature file appended to your outgoing email? Do press releases available online quote you correctly?

Identify targets

If you wanted to reach out to a wider audience offline, you would contact a journalist, similarly to talk to more people online, you need to get noticed by influencers like popular bloggers.

Readership of newspapers and magazines is declining by tens of percents every year. Youngsters are reading blogs often as a substitute for their daily newspaper. As people are spending more time online, that has to be the place to talk to your audience. This medium is also more interactive, a factor you need to consider when communicating here.

Public relations now need to consider social media, citizen journalists, and bloggers when disseminating company news releases. Again, start with your company website. Is there a press room there with updated information on your company, the latest news, photos and top management bios? This information should clearly tell anyone who's looking who you are, what you do, why that's important and how you can be contacted.This press room is important because it is likely to be the only place on the web where you have complete control over your information. As you share information online and others engage in the conversation, this information is amended, supplemented and may even be questioned.

Precision

Resist the urge to tell all about you company just because you have limitless space to do so on your website. The time people have to read and assimilate the information you disseminate is still limited. Respect the time of the person who has taken the trouble to come to your website. In a simple, conversational manner, convey the salient points about your company. You can have links for supplementary information which the viewer can click on, if he or she wants to.

Latest news

Share what's happening with your company using your blog. Your press releases should also be archived on your company website, so that they are easy to find. Also add an RSS feed for your press releases. Also include the most recent posts from your blog in this section. This will help make your company seem more human.

Testimonials

Include testimonials from your satisfied customers in this section. This will help to enhance your reputation. As your website is the one space for you to showcase your company, specific instances of customer satisfaction straight from the horse's mouth will add to your company perception. Even though these testimonials would be all positive, being on your site, they would still go a long way in building your company aura.

Multiple media

Take advantage of the fact that you can provide content in a variety of rich formats. Logos, videos, high resolution images of executives and products should all be present here. These are often needed by journalists and bloggers. If these are not easily available, communicators in a hurry may skip featuring you on their articles.

Ensure you include any media by a third party which portrays you in a transparent manner. Did your chief executive plant a tree in support of a cause? Upload the footage on your site. Did an e-paper do a podcast interview with company management? Make downloading the podcast or listening to it online possible.

Key points to ORM

Authenticity

It is very important to be honest online. Although it may seem easy to assume an identity online, your response to consumers online needs to be transparent. In case someone discovers that you were using a fake identity, the resulting fallout could be extremely unpleasant.

Integrating

Do you have an existing reputation management plan? Or is it part of your crisis management plan? Include trawling the internet for negative comments and tapping social media to enhance your perception.

Research

Finding out what's there about you online, conversing with others online to influence your reputation and search optimization knowledge is what you need to rise to the top of the online popularity charts.

Effort

The time taken for your online reputation management plan to see results depends on the size of your company. Bigger companies are written about more, smaller companies may be more niches, with more content being generated about them on specialist forums. It also depends on how intensively you want to track what is being said about you online. Basic online reputation management tools are available, but if you have a clear idea of what you wish to do on social media, it may take you more time to set up shop online. It may seem like monitoring your reputation online is a task that you don't have time for and wish to delegate. A word of caution- as discussed, authenticity is key online- outsourcing your online responses to manage your reputation online may dilute your unique voice.

Monitoring and planning your online reputation

What should you monitor?

Your own brands, communication, competition, industry trends and any weaknesses you may have.

Your own brands

Ensure you track all the possible ways in which your company and brand name can be spelt. Also track company spokespersons.

Your marketing campaigns

You can track the spread of your marketing campaign online from a single link to multiple blogs and news sites.

Where should you monitor?

Casting a wide net

If you don't know which sites your audience tends to use, you may consider tracking keywords.

Finding centres of influence

This involves a little more work upfront. Identify the online special interest groups, social networks and blogs which are patronized by your audience. These sites will be unique to your industry. This will help you refine and target your monitoring.

Ask your customers

Solicit feedback from your audience when they visit you in the form of an online survey, follow up email or live chat.

Sort your RSS feeds by date updated

This lets you know how a conversation is spreading across sites.

Monitoring your online reputation

RSS Reader

This aggregates RSS feeds, like Google Reader (google.com/reader). It is free and lets you create folders to manage different RSS feeds- All feeds related to your corporate name are automatically added in a corporate folder. Or, you could sort feeds according to whether they appeared on a blog, a social network and so on.

Conversation channels you should consider tracking

You should consider tracking Google's network, blogs, multimedia content, forums , message boards and consumer reviews and effectively utilize Web analytics.

If you are tracking keyword phrases, use quotation marks so that search engines can consider them as one entry. You can also try negative matching; use a - sign to indicate which word to ignore when it occurs with a keyword.

See if blogs have an RSS feed only for comments, which you can search for relevant comments. You could use blogpulse.com/conversation to track the spread of a conversation from a single blog. Enter the blog post URL and keyword. Use the resulting RSS feed to see which blogs link to the original and discuss the keyword. Many conversation sites offer RSS feed to track your name in discussions, like Yahoo! Answers. Enter your keyword in the search box and subscribe to the resultant feed. You could follow a similar procedure for social bookmarking sites. It is not easy to track videos and photos beyond Google Videos in Google Alerts because they do not use text.

Use copernicus.com or boardtracker.com to track mention in forum conversations. RSS feed options are generally not available on these forums. For tracking customer reviews you may need the appropriate software. Use web analytics like Google Analytics to see what search terms are bringing visitors to your site. Individual blogs may not show up but aggregators like Digg or Technorati will.

A change to your top entry page may indicate a new conversation. If visitors usually come to the home page first, but you see a spurt in visitors going directly to a particular brand page, it could indicate a new conversation.

Who will make sense of this data?

Consider appointing a reputation manager or assign tasks to different departments based on the fit.

Drilling deeper in conversations

If the conversation mentioning you is part of a RSS feed, watch for the conversation continuing.

Look for new phrases to add to the keywords you monitor.

Sentiment analysis

Maintain a channel wise record of the number of positive and negative mentions to see what your online reputation is on an overall basis.

Building Online Presence

3

Having learnt where to search and how to monitor our reputation, it's time to get into action. So how do you enhance your online reputation? How do you protect it? In this chapter you'll learn about all these challenges, the action plan for enhancing ORM and how you use the apertures of ORM to build your reputation.

Enhancing your online reputation

Verify facts

Does your detractor have a legitimate case or is he or she just trying to make trouble?

Seek trusted advice

Consult your PR person, management team or friend in case of a crisis.

Check the potential for damage

See whether the conversation is continuing, how influential are the people talking and how prestigious are the sites where these conversations are occurring.

Know your detractor

Is your detractor in the habit of complaining online? How has he or she been appeased in the past?

What should your response to a valid attack be?

1. The response should come from your top management

2. Acknowledge any mistake you may have made and make an apology

3. Ensure the dialogue is hosted by you

4. Work towards a solution

The response should come from your top management

Don't involve your PR team in your response to a detractor. You will be perceived as not taking the issue seriously enough. Use a top ranking official's name even if he does not deliver the message personally. You need to make it seem that the crisis is important enough to justify a reply from a senior manager.

Acknowledge any mistakes you may have made and make an apology

Once you've decided who should respond, the next step is deciding what he or she should say. If you have goofed up, don't hide the fact. Explain how it could have happened, what remedial steps you are taking and the preventive measure you are putting in place to ensure the incident is not repeated. The very fact that you are keeping communication lines open during this time will improve your image.

Ensure the dialogue is hosted by you

If you respond to your critic on his or her blog, he or she may take time to approve your comment, edit it or even choose not to publish it. Rather than responding to many negative comments on an individual basis, conduct the conversation on your website.

This will give you more control over the issue. Consider sharing your contact number to show that you are open to a direct conversation with your critics. You could also think about offering to be interviewed by the detractor or in case you think he or she is biased, by a respected industry blogger.

Work towards a solution

If your detractor has a valid complaint, identify what you can do to make him or her withdraw it. Offer that and ensure that the negative post against you is deleted.

Your critic should become your evangelist

Negative word of mouth spreads faster than positive feedback. A critic who has had his complaint resolved satisfactorily will spread this news the fastest.

How do you protect your reputation?

Make personal contact

In case your email or comment is not followed by removal of the defamation, try calling them. In case a number is not given, you may find the site owner and phone number at the official WHOIS domain name registry. Domaintools.com is one such website offering this service.

Send the correct information

Anytime you see anything incorrect being said about your company or brand online, try sending across accurate information. Most publishers will correct their posts.

Ask for a full retraction and apology

Ask for the incorrect post to be deleted so that it doesn't appear in Google. Just as you need to apologize if it is a mistake on your part, ask the publisher to tender a public apology. This will be something you can link to in case the issue ever gets reported again.

Contact influencers

As the conversation spreads with wrong information, clarify your standpoint not only to the original publisher but also to those who have joined the conversation.

Legal steps

In case the publisher refuses to correct the information he or she has published, contact your lawyer.

Share your side of the story

Publish an official response on your site so that Google, media and other stakeholders can access it when necessary.

Cleaning up your reputation on Google

Monitor the first 30 results for keywords concerning you on Google. Although your audience will view the first 10 results generally, you can keep an eye on potential trouble makers if you view the first 30 results.

Physical removal by your detractor

In case your detractor refuses to delete the offending post, ask him or her to change the title, or add a clarification to the beginning of the post. This will have more chances of showing up on Google, which tracks the first few sentences on a web page.

Action plan for ORM

1. Stakeholders analysis

These include your customers, media, industry opinion leaders, communities, detractors. Pen down the importance level of each for your reputation. This would include asking your stakeholders what they think about you and also collecting what they have written about you, your corporate and your brands. You could use online forums for this.

2. Online SWOT analysis

Uncover your internal reputation assets and liabilities , online content channels and your identity.

3. Craft strategy

Write your goals - include short and long term goals. Your starting point should be the results of your reputation audit. craft a strategy and write objectives

4. Implement

Create an implementation plan, sample implementation plan - Set yourself timeline and assign responsibility owners for achieving your goals.

5. Feedback

Build a Plan to Sustain Your Reputation

Points of Presence

Social networking

Social networks allow you to build deep emotional connections with your audience. However, first you need to check whether your audience is present on social networking sites.

Is a Twitter or Facebook account enough?

Once you've created a Facebook account, keep updating it intelligently so that your users find it useful to stay connected with you. The more friends you have, the more reputable you will seem to your stakeholders. The friends you have on social networking sites will serve as brand advocates.

Focus more on your brand than on your products or services. Obvious product promotion may result in people not even bothering to read your message fully. Additionally, people may prefer a more fun, unofficial Facebook profile to your official one.

Be upfront about your motive for being present on a social networking site. Post why you are there, what you are looking for from your stakeholders, with emphasis on what you plan on giving in return.

Make it easy for your stakeholders to connect with the brand. Interesting games and exciting contests build a positive brand sentiment in the minds of your network of friends. On their next visit to the store, your brand may be on the top of their mind.

Remember that every act of yours has an impact on your reputation. If you announce a contest and then cancel it, your community is likely to criticize you.

Pillars of social networking

1. Build your social networking profile

Include a description of your company or your bio. Ensure you also incorporate multimedia content like video and images. The more friends you have on social networks, the greater your online reputation will be.

2. Target multiple sites

Consider building your profile on many social networking sites to tap audiences of differing profiles.

3. Be honest

As all you do on social networking sites is mostly visible to others, be careful about the people you add or the communities you join.

4. Listen

Listen to what's being said about your brand and respond. The followers of the person posting can see your response on sites like Twitter. In this manner, positive word of mouth about your speedy response time is likely to spread.

5. Think content over numbers

Number of followers alone does not build reputation. The kind of content you share is also important in building regard.

Individuals will also benefit from being present on social networking sites like LinkedIn. For Twitter, take advantage of its nature. It's short, speedy updates result in many people accessing it while they are on the go.Tweet industry news as it happens. This will help you build a reputation of knowing about important things. Cross blog here so that your followers on Twitter can also read your blog. Content is easily available when you are at conferences, industry events or trade shows, so ensure that you are logged in to Twitter from these locations. Twitter is also a great place for you as a company to broadcast urgent announcements. You can also ask your stakeholders questions here, which they can answer instantly on Twitter. Keep an eye on what important bloggers and journalists are tweeting.

Sources of web content under your control

1. Your company website

Google algorithms allow display of two pages from a site. While your home page is likely to be picked up, don't leave the decision of the second page to be featured from your site to Google. You could try to ensure your 'About Us' page gets featured as the second link.

2. Corporate subdomains

One way of getting around Google's two page limit from a site is to use company subdomains. This will ensure the reputation of your main site helps your subdomains too. However, Google demands the content on these subdomains should be extensive and also different from the main corporate site. Your careers section or customer support should meet these criteria. Even with a subdomain, you must ensure that there are relevant incoming links.

3. Additional corporate websites

One website may not be enough for all your content. In case of a diverse line of business, multiple websites may be the solution. As in the case of subdomains, Google requires the content on these websites to be different from your main company site. You could create a website for your corporate social responsibility initiatives. Alternatively, you could have a customer forum where your customers could discuss ideas.

4. Company blog

You can have a separate URL for your corporate blog. Visitors may not go to your primary site then, but your chances of occupying another position on the top page of Google search results for your brand go up. Direct2dell.com is a good example of how to launch a corporate blog on another website in a successful manner.

5. Maintain a presence on social networks

Ensure that your company's name is the profile name, not your personal name. This may too show up well in search engine results for your brand. LinkedIn is a good place to start as it is a business network.

6. Wiki entry

If your company is large, it may already have a Wikipedia entry. That is likely to do well in search engine results for your brand. Even if your company is too new to merit a Wikipedia entry, you could consider using other wiki options. Aboutus.org is an editable guide to websites. You could also try wetpaint.com which lets you create a wiki and gives you a subdomain name. You could also encourage users to contribute to your wetpaint page. Alternatively, if you want to use wetpaint to boost your search engine rankings, you can restrict contributions by users by selecting the users who you wish to add to your wetpaint wiki.

Become a volunteer editor with Wikipedia. Sign up for a profile there and share information on yourself, while keeping track of the edits you make to the site. As Google favors Wikipedia, there is a good chance your Wikipedia profile will make its top ten search results when someone is looking for you online. However, bear in mind that for your Wikipedia profile to move to Google's first page, you need to be an active editor. You could try making several small changes to many articles in your field, rather than making a few big changes to articles on subjects that interest you. Although this may involve more work, your profile page is likely to rank well as a result.

7. Conference and seminars

If your company takes part in a seminar or a conference, it is likely that the organizers will provide you with a profile page. Ensure the keywords you want to appear in Google search results are used here. You can then link to this page from your company website.

8. Industry associations

If your company is a member of an industry association or city chamber of commerce, ask if there is a page available for you to add your company details. As most associations' web pages are highly regarded, a new page would also benefit from this trust. Your information here could then be part of the top ten search results on Google more rapidly than via a social networking profile.

Once you've fine tuned the top ten results on Google when your company is searched for, keep an eye out for new sites, developments and social networks. The top ten search results for your company may change with time, so it is imperative that you monitor your search results.

Blogging

Be committed when you launch a blog. Pay attention to the software and template you use and your writing style to engage your readers.

Blogging is a means of direct communication to your audience. Hence it is deeply personal in nature and power. It is also a means of optimizing search engine results. Media persons often read blogs for story ideas, so your blog will also enable you to reach media more rapidly.

While writing your blog, simultaneously you must make it known that your blog exists. There is little point in writing a blog if you are the only person reading it.

Brand building with blogs

Why is building your brand with a blog such a great idea? More and more people are reading blogs now.

A blog can function as a connector between all the diverse people who know you and their varied business agendas towards your company. It can spark off a conversation between these diverse stakeholders about your company.

The more personal nature of blogs also results in them resonating with consumers better than websites.

Blogging benefits for corporates and brands

Informal company communication

A corporate blog is a speedy way of reaching out to people beyond your potential audience. Unlike in a press release where you would co ordinate with a PR person, who would share the release with media and then your audience would read it, with a blog you can simultaneously reach out to all these three categories.

Customer feedback channel

A corporate blog, is a two way communication channel. Allow comments on your blog for consumers to share opinions on your products, communication and service.

Even if you receive some negative comments, look upon that as an opportunity to react in a transparent and professional manner. You may convert a dis-satisfied customer in a brand evangelist. Also, it is better to be aware of such a comment on your blog, rather than have it floating around online where you may be oblivious to it.

Creating customer value

Treat your blog like any other product offering in your portfolio. Ensure you maintain the same high level of quality across your blog posts.

Select your blog writing style

Match your blog writing style to the personality you want to come through in the blog. If your blog is authentic, well written and geared to customer needs, the style is immaterial. Ensure that once you have decided on your writing style you maintain it. A transparent, interactive blog that chooses to keep quiet during a corporate crisis will lose your readers' respect.

The Individual expert blog

The expert blog is an opportunity for you to establish yourself as a specialist. This reputation will hold you in good stead even if you change companies. The company may benefit in an indirect manner from your writing. These blog posts are not officially endorsed by the company.

Before starting your expert blog, crosscheck with your employer that there are no company restrictions on you writing about the domain the company operates in.

The corporate executive blog

Usually written by the CEO or some other high ranking company official, these kind of blogs help put a human face to the company. It is often a pleasant surprise to readers that the CEO of a company can be so accessible.

Ensure that your CEO personally writes the blog; else it could lose its impact. He or she may write posts while travelling, or email posts to a company administrator to upload online. The frequency of these posts may even be monthly. Of course, frequent blogging will increase reader engagement. Take care that posting frequency is consistent, however. A caveat- your CEO should be willing to blog. If he or she is unable to write posts of substance due to security reasons, it is better not to have this kind of a blog.

The company team blog

Written in a collaborative blog style, this type of blog has posts from many employees. Readers would get a better sense of an organization when employees lower down in the hierarchy share their opinions. You could have various issues covered in this blog, which could be written by the most suitable employee. Also, the time taken to write posts is distributed among many employees, improving frequency of posting. Employees should be encouraged to post freely, but must adhere to a process.

The corporate update blog

Posts on this blog type would offer real time, correct information on company status and products. The frequency would be as and when required. You should still maintain a transparent, natural tone. Reader comments would continue to offer you valued inputs.

Choosing your blog platform

The software takes care of the creative look of the page, the components and the creation of every blog post page. Choose carefully as it is not easy to change your blog software solution after you start using a particular one.

Developer hosted blog software

Blogs hosted by the developer reside on the software provider's servers and require no installation by you. Blogger.com, typepad.com and wordpress.com are some available developer hosted blog software solutions. These save you the hassle of server configurations or manually updating your blog software.

Wordpress.com and blogger.com are free and easy to use. They also provide options for design customization, comments and categories or tagging. Individuals or small businesses would do well to use this option.

User Hosted Blog Software

These take more time and effort to deploy but are more flexible. Drupal.org, movable-type.com, wordpress.org are some examples. You need to upload and install the software on your own server. This requires you to know some web programming, database management systems and hosting configurations.

Wordpress and Drupal are free and extensively supported by both the creators of the software and the blogging community that uses them. Wordpress is popular and balances usability with customization.

Why should you use user hosted blog software? There are more programming and design options or plug-ins available to you. Benefits include better SEO, the ability to achieve a closer look to your company site and added security as the files are stored on your servers.

Selecting your blog location

Choose carefully as readers and search engines know where to go online to read your blog with this URL. If you need to change this domain name later, you could erode your brand equity.

Locating your blog on the bloghost

Developer hosted blogs give you a free URL which is a subdomain. For instance, yourblog.blogger.com.

Although this is a convenient option, with SEO benefits of a reputed subdomain, your blog identity could be more distinct.

Locating your blog on your corporate website

As you need to host your user hosted blog solution on a server in any case, you may as well do so on the server you use to host your corporate site. If your blog is here it will seem related to your corporate brand too.

In this case, you have two options- subdirectory and subdomain. With a subdomain your blog URL would be along the lines of blog.yourcompany.com. The subdirectory option will give you a blog URL in the format yourcompany.com/blog. Go for a subdomain if you want Google to consider your blog as an entity which is separate from your company, while still reaping the benefits of your corporate reputation. Choose a subdirectory if you want your main site to benefit from the additional pages the blog will provide to search engines. This is a good option for company blogs.

Locate it at a separate blog domain

To create a long lasting blog brand, think about buying a separate URL. Individuals can use their own name, corporates can use a name that references their company or is creative.

SEO payoffs may not result with an individual blog URL, but there are other advantages. Bloggers will be more inclined to link to you as you will be perceived to be more independent of your company in this case. This is another way to increase your blog's popularity, which will help it to rise on Google search results.

Company executive or company team blogs and even individual expert blogs would benefit the most from this kind of a blog.

A good blog must have good blogging elements. It should have a clever blog name. Use an industry related keyword in your blog name and URL to influence your Google ranking.

Use Keyword rich page file names

Ascertain whether your blog uses the title of your blog post as the naming convention for post pages. Several blogs use a default format for each blog post URL that resembles yourblog.com/post-786. Check whether you can make this a more Google savvy format like yourblog.com/post-title.

Use unique title tags

Many blogs let you make changes to the design template or use a plug-in ensuring that every blog page has a unique title tag. The most convenient option is to instruct your blog software to use the same headline of the blog post as the title tag for the page.

Engaging Users

Subscribe to RSS feed

Have a prominent text link or graphic to allow readers to subscribe to the site's RSS feed.

Subscribe by email

For more traditional readers, provide subscribe by email option. Feedblitz.com and Feedburner.com both offer this option.

Share using social bookmarking links

Each of your blog posts should also have links enabling readers to share that item with their friends using their bookmarks on sites like delicious and Digg.com. News readers may visit your blog, trusting their friend's opinion.

Welcome comments

Comment moderation

Most blog solutions let you screen comments before they are published on your blog. Resist the temptation to disregard negative comments as that will jeopardize your reputation of being transparent. Instead, discard language that is abusive, off topic outpourings or competitor attempts at sabotage.

Spam filtration

Consider installing a plug in that monitors and deletes spam comments.

Creation of a comment policy

Publish this on your blog so that users are aware of what is welcome and what is not where comments are concerned. You could mention that abusive language, personal attacks or off topic links are unwelcome, as are anonymous comments.

Explain who you are

Don't assume all visitors to your blog know about you. Have an 'About Us' section or an 'About Me' section in case of an individual. Here you could consider including a concise business bio about career accomplishments or expertise.

An approachable photo will help readers to visually establish a connection with you. Explain to your readers if it is a company team blog or a company update blog and tell them who the contributors are, what would be the posting frequency and discussion topics.

Incorporate other media

Enable readers to share content in their preferred format by having multimedia on your blog.

Blogging Guidelines

Don't delete a blog post

After you publish a post, it will be archived elsewhere in any case. In case you have made a mistake or changed your position it's more transparent to keep your post and use notations to show changes. Deleting your post can seem suspicious and hurt your reputation.

Link to original sources of information

Your readers see you as being honest enough to share all information by your being unafraid enough to point them to another website.

Remember to disclose conflicts of interest or business relationships

Don't think that such discloses will devalue your posts. Rather, you will be perceived to be more transparent.

Involving PR and legal departments

Take their advice to help you improve upon your corporate blogging guidelines. Involving them at the beginning will enable you to stay on target as far as the company message is concerned.

Notify them as soon as you publish new blog posts, but their involvement in your blog beyond that should be minimal, or it may slow you down when it comes to posting.

Consider involving a blog manager to do these tasks.

Rules for Transparent Blogging

Your blog is your brand

Resist the temptation to be too casual in your use of language or in the issues you decide. Remember people are judging you on the basis of what you write and how you write.

Break news first

Isn't it better to have bad news where you can keep an eye on the fallout? Negative news in which your company is involved need not be the only information you link to. Showcase positive news too. Confronting the problem head on will earn you the admiration of the blogosphere.

Your blog should be the first place people visit for news concerning you. If you feature both good and bad news, your reputation for authenticity will be enhanced. People are then less likely to believe what others say about you.

Acknowledge peers

Don't consider peers as competition alone. Your audience is aware of the existence of both you and your competition. You could try comparing your products with that of your competition's to further enhance your reputation of being transparent.

One reason why companies fear sharing information online is because they feel their competition will have access to it. Just as you have an idea of your competitors news, wouldn't they too know what the new developments on your front are?

You may also not want to share your expertise online but doing so will increase your market value, not reduce it.

Engage readers

Assign a person in case of a company team blog to monitor comments and respond accordingly. In the case of a company executive blog, an assistant could monitor comments and bring any comments requiring a direct response to your notice.

Even if you don't have an answer, respond with a timeline on when you will have the answer.

Be consistent

Once you decide to start a blog, you need to keep it going. If you decide to discontinue, your audience will perceive this act in a negative manner.

Measuring your blog's success

Number of	Description
Visitors	Along with numbers measure time spent and quality of blog visitors statistics. Track growth and repeat visits.
Blog Mentions	Keep checking this number at regular intervals to monitor your progress in the blogosphere popularity ratings.
Web-links	This would greatly improve search engine ratings for your blog.
RSS subscribers	Lets you know how many are looking forward for latest updates.
Blog Comments	This lets you know how engaging your blog is.
Media mentions	Check if mainstream media has quoted you from your blog.
Sales	Ask new customers how they heard about you. See if any of them mention your blog.

Press releases

Your audience for your press release is no longer journalists alone. Online, it is possible for anyone to read your press release. They can then use sites like digg.com to share news. Other users vote on these items, thus creating a virtuous circle of popularity. Sites like delicious.com and stumbleupon.com are also used to store news items as social bookmarks. The content you create showcasing your area of specialization, which may be relevant to others, could find a place here.

Online press release format

Contact details

Display contact details first, unlike in a traditional press release. This enables readers to know who to contact in case they want additional information. Ensure you provide multiple means of contact which are web friendly, like instant messenger ids and email addresses. Also include your telephone number and website URL.

Tweaking the headline

As in the case of an offline press release, the headline should attract your reader's attention. However, your online press release should also get noticed by search engines and potential clients. So you must include words that resonate with your customer and keywords that will come up in search engines.

Key news facts

Instead of the usual introduction and body, arrange the information you wish to share using bullet points. Readers online prefer this mode of communication to paragraphs.

RSS feed and links to a customized page

Online, it is possible for you to include more updated content using links and RSS feeds. A link could lead to a page online which has supplementary information on market trends, news and analysis.

Multimedia content

Links to photos, videos and podcasts should be embedded in your online press release. This will enable the reader to conveniently gather all the material he needs to amplify your message. Additional multimedia links can take him or her to more such items which are in your pressroom.

Quotes

Offline press release scatter quotes from various company employees throughout the press release. However, it is advisable to collect all quotes and mark them in one section of your press release. This technique will increase the likelihood of their being used. This will lend a dimension of authenticity when your message is read by others.

Links to Other Articles

Leverage the advantage that an online press release provides- links can guide your reader to related content by others, rather than you having to share these in one press release. The reader will then himself or herself think that your news is part of a trend or that your news is borne out by research.

Boilerplate

This section remains the same- a short 'About Us' section with disclaimers if any.

Social Bookmarks and RSS Feeds

This section will enable your news to travel online by enabling sharing. Encouraging the reader to add your news to his or her RSS feed or having links to social bookmarking sites which enable him or her to share your news will make the spread of your news faster.

Making Your Press Release Search Engine Friendly

Search engines read your press releases too- determining the theme of your press release based on the frequency of words used. They then archive the press release till a user searches for information using the exact same phrase.

Choice of Words

Ensure the words you use in your press release are in everyday speech. Manufacturer speak is unlikely to be what consumers are looking for. Focus on the benefit you are providing rather than the technology you are using. This will enable you to reach a wider audience.

Leveraging your Brand

Similarly, ensure that you use your company name throughout your press release. Usually, pronouns such as 'it' or 'we' are used after the first mention of the company name. Avoid pronouns for your company as a single mention of your company is unlikely to catapult it to the top of the search engine lists. As most users don't go beyond the first page of results, it is important that you be available where they are searching for you. Also pepper your release with the names of your top executives- not pronouns.

Link Intelligently

Use the opportunity provided by your press release to link to relevant pages on your site. For instance, link the brand you mention in your press release to its webpage on your site. This improves chances of it ranking high in search results. This will have a snowball effect when news aggregator sites publish your press release.

Press Release Distribution Enhancement

Sites like indiaprwire.com or businesswireindia.com can host your press release for their audience. This will give you access to their readers or anyone who searches for you on their site.

Leveraging your press release

Once you've out your press release online, your job is far from over. Your online press release is a tool to ignite conversations with bloggers.

Finding Influential Bloggers

Merely blanket mailing your press release to hundreds of bloggers will not do. You need to selectively target those bloggers who write about your industry. How do you find out who they are?

Known Bloggers

Bloggers, who have written about your industry or competition in the past, or even those industry bloggers you follow, could be the ones to contact first.

Alexa, Compete

Use Alexa.com and Compete.com to determine the ranking of any website. Once you know which websites in your industry are the most popular, you can target them accordingly.

Using Search Engines

Search for popular industry blogs on search engines or on Google Blog Search, which only searches blogs.

Mainstream media

When you've shortlisted the bloggers you plan to contact, check how newsworthy they are. Search for them on Google News or Yahoo! News. Also search for them on popular search engines to see whether mainline media has quoted them. Check which bloggers your shortlisted bloggers link to on heir blogs, for further blogs to target.

Understanding blogs

Don't rush to pick up the phone to call your chosen bloggers. Take the time to read their blogs and engage with them, so that they feel that you have taken the trouble to get to know them. This will enable you to personalize your communication to them and likelihood of them agreeing to write a post on you.

Engaging with blogs

Comment on blogs in a manner which adds value to them. Rather than focusing on your agenda, bring out new dimensions to the conversation. You could also share industry news or what you feel about trends in the industry. This will ensure bloggers have a positive impression about you before you reveal your agenda.

Conversation tracking

Once a blogger writes a post on you, monitor it for any comments that are posted. A blog post is the first step in a conversation. A conversation happens between many readers discussing, debating and adding to the points put forward.

Using SEO to manage your reputation

Your challenge is to ensure that the first ten results which show up when a user does a Google search on you- are positive. One negative result could neutralize nine positive links

Being user friendly

Google suggests using words and phrases that users are likely to type when searching for you. You could also conduct a dipstick among users to find out what keywords they actually use.

Enabling Google crawling

Search engine spiders ignore page styles and images when crawling the web. Ensure that in your quest to appeal to your users you are not coming across as incomprehensible to search engine spiders.

Another way in which individual page ranks can improve is to give them a keyword name. Using a name like company.com/page_id=786/ is not as vivid as company.com/shekharkhanna if that page has your CEO's bio. This will help you to reach the top ten results in Google for that particular keyword.

Besides making sure that your web pages are named strategically, they should also be easy to navigate. A search engine spider will try to index each page on your site one by one. A page may be inaccessible if no other page links to it or if the navigation you use (like flash) is one that a search engine spider has problems with. In that case, the page is unlikely to be displayed in search results. If it's not there, a journalist will be unable to find it when he or she is writing an article on you.

Use text link navigation to enable search engine spiders to move with ease from one of your web pages to another. Use descriptive text in the link. Rather than saying 'click here', you could say 'About Shekhar Khanna'. This tells Google the page is about your CEO.

The title tag

This informs search engines what is the main theme of your web page. It is especially important because it is the first bits of information users see when your web page appears in search results. Write your title tags to also convey a positive impression. This is done even before they click on the search result. So instead of a plain 'About Us' you could write 'About Tata Steel: Trusted Innovators'. Also try to include relevant keywords in the title tag. Remember to pack what you want to say in the first few words as Google's algorithms don't consider title tags after 66 characters.

Page content

In the absence of images, search engine spiders go by content. If you make sure that each of your web pages is structured around a theme of keywords, they are more likely to show up in searches. Don't overdo it though- you may put off your target audience. A good rule of thumb is to mention your keyword as often as you would in a natural conversation.

Google page rank & incoming links

Google's Page Rank considers pages that link together to be related. Each incoming link is considered as a vote for your page. Having said that, not all links are equal. They should be in a similar space to your industry.

Your content should be such that visitors will want to share it with others- by social bookmarking or linking to it from their website.

You could also try searching for websites in your industry. Once you've identified potential links, you could attempt writing to them requesting a link to your website.

Link-baiting is also something you could try initially. Create unique, attention getting or controversial content to attract social bookmarking sites and bloggers. The resultant buzz could help you draw in many links to your site.

You could also consider contacting your business partners to link to your site.

Tools and Codes

4

ORM would involve understanding and selecting tools from service providers. You should have a content strategy which would also encompass how to utilize multimedia content. This chapter takes you through content strategies and a description of famous ORM tools.

Codes of Communication

Creating engaging content

Content creating is important to drown out any negatives that Google picks up. The more positive content you create and put online, the more likely that one negative comment will be sidelined. Creating content also allows you to control that content, rather than being controlled by what someone else writes, which may or may not be positive.

How to write reputation enhancing content

Offline, you may well write using an introduction, body and conclusion. Online, it is more beneficial if you organize your information using links. Many readers online simply scan articles rather than read them word by word. Other ways to organize your text are using bullets, highlighting words and sub headlines.

Writing White Papers and Online Books

While using Twitter may be good for updating information or sharing thoughts in real time, thought leadership needs more words. Put your research findings or arguments in a white paper. The format should be similar to the one you would use when writing for print media. Upload it on your website as HTML so that search engines can track it down and index it. Also upload a PDF version for users to download and print. You could also post these useful articles on your blog or ask other influencers online to post a link on their blogs.Once your reputation has been built using white papers, you can supplement it with shorter, timely blog posts.

An online book is also a good way to showcase your competency. You could self publish at lulu.com or upload the book on your site.

Be clear

Use short, crisp sentences to get your point across. People read more slowly online, so make it easyfor them to understand what you are saying. Resist the temptation to show off by using jargon.

Be professional

Remember to use correct grammar in your communication. Otherwise, you may put off your audience. Make good use of Microsoft Word's spell check and grammar check.

Be engaging

Gear your content towards your reader by putting him or her at the centre. What does he or she want? How can you help? The overlap between your expertise and your audience's needs is where engagement happens.

Provide new content as much as possible, rather than links to other content online, which others are likely to be linking to as well. The fresher the content, the more likely you are to elicit a response from your reader in the form of a comment.

Be passionate about what you are saying. Once you have announced your area of expertise, offer your opinion on any developments there in a memorable manner.

Ensure your personality comes through when you write. This will happen anyway if you are honest. It helps your writing seem consistent. Recall will also improve. A humorous tone will engage your audience more as it will seem personal.

Ask your readers to participate by highlighting the available means to do so. Use questions while writing and ask for responses from readers in those areas. Invite comments, links, video posts, photo posts and bookmarks.

Use the testimonials you get to their full advantage. Post appreciative emails on your site or ask the writer to post the email as a comment on your blog or site. Users value feedback from people like them more than what they perceive to be interested parties.

Use your headlines

First impressions matter and a headline is the first impression readers have of you. That is what they will read first on Google search results or on social bookmarking sites. A headline should describe and interest while having an element of intrigue. Once the reader's curiosity is sparked, he or she will be compelled to read further.

Voice

Use active voice more than passive voice to sound more direct, strong and engaging.

You can use first person, second person or third person in your narrative style. The first person will make you sound more important than your reader. The third person is impersonal and too formal for online usage. Neither does it engage your reader as much as the second person. The second person scores because the reader is at the centre.

Storytelling

Use storytelling to attract your audience. Stories usually revolve around a moral or values. These are at the centre of any individual or company. As these are important to build your reputation, structure your corporate social responsibility acts in the format of a story rather than a company statement. This will involve your readers more than a bald company statement.

Position your company as the hero and look for the crisis which needed to be solved. The crisis could be your competitor, the government's new regulation, game changing technology or an economic disaster. Make the means of solving the problem the company values. These values should ideally be constant over time. You could also involve your customers. Encourage them to tell stories of when they were able to surmount obstacles using your products.

Your 'About Us' page

A great place to showcase your story is your About Us page. Build a relationship with your audience here by using images, videos and sound. Get your readers to feel that they are getting to know the real you by providing the inside story on the way you work, your challenges and triumphs.

Email

Email is more in the control of the receiver- he or she could delete your mail without even reading it. Or, it may go in the spam folder. To prevent this, ensure that your email is relevant to your recipient.

Why are you sending the email? What do you want the receiver to do? You could be informing the receiver about a new white paper and wanting him or her to download it.

People expect a speedy response to an email. If you will take longer than 48 hours to revert, mention that on your website.

Ensure that you are not irritating your receiver. If you intend to enhance your reputation, unless you are authentic and demonstrate attention to your recipient's needs, you may come across as dispensing corporate spin.

Your return address

Your return address can serve as a branding tool. The best email address is yourname@yourcompany.com. Using your name in your address tells receivers who you are and is corporate protocol.

Subject line

As email recipients look at the return address or the subject line first, be upfront about the reason for the mail in the subject line itself. Include your brand name here.

Message content

Come to the point quickly. Try to greet your recipient by name if possible. This will aid you in building a relationship with him or her. Elaborate on the reason for the email. End with a call to action and your signoff.

Signature file

Your signature file is a permanent way to build your reputation. Include your contact information and designation.You could also include links to blogs, website, and Flickr photos.Consider mentioning calls to action like subscribing to RSS feed. A brand statement, corporate news or new launch announcements are other items you could incorporate.

A quote related to your line of business could also make memorable reading.Ensure your signature file is text alone because some email programs block images. Consider customizing your signature file according to your audience. Avoid legalese in your signature file as most receivers do not read it. Neither does it help in building your reputation. Email newsletters must have information on how to unsubscribe.

Instant messaging

Use instant messaging if you are mostly online. Ensure you update your status in case you are not. You could also include your screen name on your business card. Ensure that your screen name is a professional one.

Multimedia content usage for audience engagement

Do you have a knowledge niche? Use multimedia content to showcase this knowledge to the best advantage. Even if you are a small company, you can make an impact by providing insights that people find useful. Ensure you display this knowledge in appropriate places like Wikipedia.

What comes in multimedia? Text, images, audio and video all comprise multimedia. Social media is an ideal place to host your multimedia content.

An image speaks more than words

Do your images convey the true nature of your company? Carry a digicam to company events or conferences which your company is participating in to keep updating available images online. Encourage employees to capture images that reflect the company ethos.

Consider your office images. Do they focus on the building only or are employees inside the office in the frame as well? The latter will make the image come alive.

What image do your head shots convey? Do you want to communicate creativity, reliability or friendliness? Choose with care.

Social media and images

You can use an online photo hosting site like Photobucket to store your photos till they are needed. By linking to them from your website or your outgoing email, they will register in the minds of a wider audience. A site like Flickr, which is associated with Yahoo, is likely to reap you benefits in search engine results for your brand, if you host your images there. Facilitate posting of images where your customers are using your products. Post them after you approve them, on your website. You could add casual employee images to your 'About Us' section. Also ensure that blogs and community sites have these kinds of images posted by your users.

Videos speak more than images

Using videos is especially important if your audience is young, as more youngsters watch videos. You can have video reviews of your products, demonstrations and post your commercials on YouTube. Have an overlay or a watermark with your URL on these videos. This will enable you to have copyright control and promote content even if it leaves these sites.

Facilitate posting of images where your customers are using your products. Post them after you approve them, on your website. You could add casual employee images to your 'About Us' section. Also ensure that blogs and community site have these kinds of images posted by your users.

Virtual tours

Another way to enhance your transparency is to have a virtual tour of your facilities. A virtual tour is a simulation of an existing location, usually composed of a sequence of video images. They also may use other multimedia elements such as sound effects, music, narration, and text. Such virtual tours are made up of a number of shots taken from a single vantage point. A video tour is a full motion video of a location. Unlike the virtual tour's static wrap-around feel, a video tour is as if you were walking through a location. Using a video camera, the location is filmed while moving from place to place. Video tours are continuous movement taken at a walking pace.

Talking head videos

Ensure you harness the potential of this medium by having videos which have movement, rather than simply a person talking.

Social Media and videos

Videos are a great way to spread content virally as many users share videos they find interesting with their friends. You could also ask customers to create videos showing them using your products. Even if some feedback is negative it will only help you to improve your offering. You will seem more open in the process. You could run a contest to motivate users to upload videos.

SEO for Multimedia

As search engines focus on text, it is difficult for them to track multimedia. Make their job easier by using appropriate file names, tags and titles. Also ensure that the context in which they are displayed is relevant- like your blog or site. Try to include your company name and location in the title and also mention the content of the video- the situation it is depicting.

Technorati search engines look at tagging, so pay special attention to tagging your content with multiple tags so that it shows up in all related keyword searches. Use tags with multiple words as that is often how users search. Also consider using abbreviations in your tags if that is more popular than the full form. Make sure you include synonyms that are often used in your tags as well.

Think about sharing slides from your latest PowerPoint presentation at a seminar online at slideshare.net. You will score points for letting it be known that you were invited to the seminar to speak, but you will come across as more open if you share your content.

You could also use WebEx to run a webinar. This will enable interested clients to sample your offerings or share your knowledge, even if they are in far flung locations. Remember to include engaging features like a poll online with an instant report, automatic follow up mails and interactive panels.

Consider establishing a presence online at Second Life. Wipro, Satyam and Tata Indicom have all done so. Wipro has conducted webinars here and Tata Indicom has launched a promotion.

Micromedia content

Share small bytes of content while you are on the move via sites like Twitter. Any information snippet that you come across that could enhance your reputation as a knowledge provider could be uploaded.

Engaging viewers with audio

Using audio on your site is advisable if you are in a related field. Else, it may distract visitors. If you have knowledge to share, podcasts may be the answer.

Tools and Apertures

ORM Tools

Given below is a list of ORM tools that enables monitoring features. Each has its own unique advantages and hence a decision about which tool to be used should be made after understanding how each one works.

Some of the tools provide features for classifying the conversations as positive , negative and neutral.

Points of Action

Action Point 1

Brand monitoring tool scours the entire web for mentions of your brands in various blogs and user communities.

Action Point 2

The brand buzz is then categorized as per your agreement with your Social Media partner. It could be as general as positive, negative and neutral sentiments or as specific as to which user is spreading negativities about your brand.

Action Point 3

The important conversations are grouped under various heads as per the seriousness of the incidents so that you can take remedial action.

Brand monitoring is slowly picking up in Indian companies; many brands have a dedicated budget for this niche Social Media programme.

Before deep diving in Social Media programmes, it is best to deploy free Social Media tools to understand the overall sentiments about your brand.

ORM tools to listen to conversations about your brand

Google Alerts
http://www.google.com/alerts

Google Alerts cover "News", "Web", "Blogs", "Groups" and "Video".
A Google alert lets you know if:

- News search - New articles make it into the top ten news results.
- Web search - New web pages appear in the top twenty results.
- Blog search - New blog posts make it into the top ten results
- Groups search - New group posts make it into the top fifty results.
- Video search - New videos make it into the top ten results.

A sixth type of Google Alert, "Comprehensive", combines the results of the Google Alerts for "News", "Web" and "Blogs".
Setting up Google Alerts means you get updates automatically as they happen without having to run manual searches repeatedly yourself.

Google Trends
http://www.google.com/trends

Google Trends delivers charts that show how often a particular search term or terms are entered relative to the total search volume across regions of the world, and in various languages.
Popularity is broken down by region, city and language, and it's possible to refine the main graph by region and time period.

Google Blog Search
http://blogsearch.google.com

Use this tool to search amongst pools of blogs around the globe. Google Blog Search can be initiated simply by entering keywords and phrases in the search box, or honed with the advanced search facility available from the Google Blog Search homepage.

Technorati
http://www.technorati.com

The first blog search service, Technorati is still considered by many to be the best. It spiders and indexes over 112 million blogs, the results can be sorted by "authority" and "rank".

Delicious
http://del.icio.us

Delicious is the first social bookmarking website and searching it gives you an idea of what people are bookmarking.

Other popular social bookmarking services include StumbleUpon, Magnolia.

Digg
http://www.digg.com

A social news service, Digg describes itself as follows: "Everything on Digg -from news, videos, images and podcasts-is submitted in our community. Once something is submitted, other people see it and Digg what they like best. If your submission is popular and receives enough Diggs, it is promoted to the front page for the millions of our visitors to see".

Backtype.com

If searching for your company amidst blog comments is your concern, this is the site for you.

Search.twitter.com

Use this to search for any tweets related to your business.

Trackur.com

It scours the Internet and provides extras (like charts and filters) that other sites don't. If someone is talking badly about you or your company, instead of simply taking offence and dwelling on negative comments, address them and take the criticism for what it's worth: a chance to grow and learn.

10 Social Media tracking and analytics tools

Social Mention

If you ever wonder about tracking what people are saying about you all across the web, then Social Mention is the answer. It's a search and analysis platform that collects content from across the globe into one stream of information. Through this you can easily track comments about your company/products/services. More than 100 Social Media properties, including Twitter, Facebook, FriendFeed, Digg, YouTube, are tracked through this tool. Opt for Social Mention for point-in-time search and analysis, alerts, and API.

Bit.ly

This is a web tool that shrinks long URLs, and has statistical tools to track down the popularity of shortened links. Sometimes serious work could be fun and Bit.ly is a perfect example. Simply shorten long URLs and track the real time clicks easily.

SocialToo

SocialToo can help you be a social networking power user. It lets you keep your follower lists in sync across networks, and learn more about your relationships. Features include- creating surveys and sending them to multiple networks, tracking Social Media stats, auto follow, auto filtering and much more. You will also get daily e-mail on who is following you and who unfollows you on Twitter.

Twitteranalyzer

It is an interesting tool that helps to get all kinds of statistical charts about you and your friends' behavior on Twitter. Some features of this tool are similar to Google Analytics. Some of its exciting features are - you can see how many followers are online presently, who retweets your messages, what people are writing about you, Twitter following stats, your Tweeting habits and many more.

Xinureturns

This is one of the best Social Media tracking tools to get a dashboard overview of your website on social networks and search engines. To get comprehensive info on Social Bookmarks, Technorati, Indexed Page, Google Pagerank, Ranking- all you have to do is to run this report.

Tweetstats

Tweetstats helps you analyze your tweets in various ways in the form of graphs. You will receive a graphic representation of your tweets/hour, tweets/month, tweet timeline and reply statistics. Now if you wish to have a graph of "Today's Top 10 Twitter Apps" and "Today Top @'ed Tweeps", you can do so easily. To run a check on which are the words that you use the most in your tweets, go to TrendCloud.

Twitalyzer

Twitalyzer is a free tool to evaluate the activity of any Twitter user and report on dozens of useful measures of success in Social Media. This is a very effective tool that gives a straight report on the behaviour of the user through his/her virtual influence and use of other tools. Links to URLs, the signal-to-noise ratio, clout, generosity and the tendency to share good information can be gauged easily.

BlogPulse

This is a very effective tool for "buzz tracking". Blog Pulse Trend Search allows you to create graphs that visually track "buzz" over time for certain key words, phrases or links and compare search terms/links in isolation, or use all three fields to compare search terms/links against others. You can use the Trend search to create your own graphs that plot "buzz" about specific search terms (issues, people, companies, brands, sports, etc.) in the blogosphere. You can also choose from three different time parameters- one month, two months or six months.

PostRank

Originally known as AideRSS it monitors and collects social engagement events correlated with online content in real-time across the web. It collects all the story-generated comments, bookmarks, tweets and various other forms of discussion from different Social Media platforms. Use PostRank facility to collect information and use it for a more targeted communication.

Broadtracker

Forums are exhaustive and sometimes you lose complete track of your presence on the threads. BoardTracker.com is the exact solution to clear such confusions. It's a forum search engine tool through which you can effectively track all the alerts, comments and other activities on the threads you are related to. You will never miss a point of discussion and you will be able to streamline information right in front of you.

Some Basic Social Media Apertures

Social Networks

Social networks allow people to build personal web pages and then connect with friends to share content and communicate. E.g. Orkut, Facebook, MySpace, Hi5.

Facebook (26 million active users), Orkut (19 million active users) in India.

(Source —www.vizisense.com)

The successful Barrack Obama election campaign employed various Social Media tools including Facebook to forge deep and meaningful conversations with people across states.

Most people use their social networks for information search as well. By socializing one can garner interesting facts in communities like Orkut. This makes social networks the most sought after media vehicle. Facebook has become an online yellow page directory.

Blogs

Blogs or web logs are online journals, where you write for a host of people eager to consume your information and experiences in the form of text, images and videos. These sites allow great room and great versatility.

How do I create an interesting and linkable blog?
Personal brands, which can in turn add value and credibility to the corporate brand, can be created through blogs.

The blog should not be based on the company's achievements alone. The copy should be made personal, entertaining and give users a reason to return.

The blog title and headlines should be catchy and creative.

Many bloggers have a huge fan following and are opinion leaders in their area of expertise. Apart from the immediate influencees (family, friends) bloggers have immense influence over potential buyers of products or services.

Wikis

Wikis allow one to not only post and access content but also revise and update content. Wikis add a new dimension to information-sharing by giving a new meaning to the term 'shared workspace'.

Wikipedia has become the first source of information for students and professionals alike. It is an easy and accessible resource for primary research. Companies like GE have an internal Wikipedia for their employees.

Content communities

There are different community groups which share a specific kind of content. For example, Flickr is formed around sharing photographs and YouTube is a video sharing community.

Like social networks, one has to register, get a home page and make connections with friends. However, they are focused on sharing a particular type of content.

Microblogging

Social networking combined with bite-sized blogging, where small amounts of content ('updates') are distributed online and through the mobile phone network. Twitter is the clear leader in this field.

Podcasts

Podcasts are audio or video files that users can subscribe to. They are published on the Internet and it is the subscription feature that makes podcasts so powerful as a form of Social Media.

When a new podcast is posted to the web, all the subscribers' podcast services (such as iTunes) are automatically notified and hence get downloaded to their computer's hard drive. One can either listen to podcast on the computer system or download to an external MP3 drive such as an iPod.

Forums/Groups

Forums commonly exist around specific topics and interests, for example cars or music. Each discussion in a forum is known as a thread, and many different threads can be active simultaneously.

This makes forums good places to find and engage in a variety of detailed discussions. Forums can be places for lively, vociferous debate, for seeking advice on a subject, for sharing news, for flirting, or simply for whiling away time with idle chat.

The sites are moderated by an administrator, whose role it is to remove unsuitable posts or spam. A major difference between a forum and a blog is that a moderator won't be leading or guiding the discussion.

Blogs have a clear owner, whereas a forum's threads are started by its members.

A peep into popular social networks

Orkut

The inherent human need to make friends led to the popularity of this social network. In India it still takes courage to initiate a conversation with a stranger. Orkut solved this need and hence its use spread like wildfire. Communities are normally made on interesting individuals i.e. bosses, heads of organization. Maintain a good profile page and monitor the community featuring your organization. Encourage the individual owning and moderating the community for greater social presence.

Facebook

Contacts can be imported from Outlook, Windows Live contacts, or searched via a specific school, university or company. The site also recommends new connections based on one's own network and information. One's profile can contain a link to the company's website.

One can post new material at least twice a week, and join and participate in groups, events; notes, photos and features can be used to keep the page current.

A business page can be created in addition to the personal page by simply clicking on "Advertising" at the bottom of any Facebook page, then "Pages", and "Create a page."

LinkedIn

This is the site to reach a skilled audience, as it allows networking among professionals.

The company recommends new contacts once one enters company information. One can also find connections by importing e-mail/address book connections.

One's profile can contain a link to one's company's site. Other apps allow one to upload and share presentations, collect data for polls and more.

It is important that the company page is maintained on regular basis by corporate communication and HR teams. Have a good description of the organization and use the network for finding right people and showcasing your organization's competence.

YouTube

Best for viral marketing based on innovative videos.Videos created by one's company can be posted to an audience of millions. The website can be linked or embedded in one's site or blog. This directs viewers to one's company. Monitoring content networks like Youtube for videos creates a channel to the organization or key individuals of the company and facilitates the release of press clippings for the desired audience.

Flickr/ Picasa

Shares visual content in a way that engages viewers. Pictures and videos can be uploaded and shared. These can be organized and tagged, which makes them easier for others to find. One can join groups and create new contacts as one becomes more involved in the site. By having individuals post their pictures and creating a database of pictures of all activities through one single id. Make the id a must see for former employees and current employees who would regularly see this link to see what their current colleagues or ex-colleagues are up to.

Twitter

One of the most popular social networking sites is Twitter which allows one to use a completely different tool called microblogging. Through Twitter, one can reach the masses very easily and effectively. İt has become a preferred advertising medium. The tweets might ignite flames that fires up controversies which are mission critical. Enter twitter in the high priority list and manage tweets about the organization as tweets reach individuals via mobile phones and create huge movements like recent İran election crisis. Have key individuals tweet regularly to showcase their connectivity and approachable naturel.

MySpace

Wove its magic by touching people through its music services offering. There are more than three million bands and musicians registered on MySpace, aiming to attract fans from among the 250 million members.

As the name suggests, social networks bring a large number of people from different nations, regions and professions under one umbrella. They create their profile page; connect with other people by inviting them or by accepting their requests and share content amongst all.

Classification of Listening tools

- radian6 social media monitoring
- Nielsen BuzzMetrics
- trackur
- BrandsEye Protecting your online reputation

- Google News
- socialmention*
- YAHOO! NEWS
- HowSociable? brand visibility metrics

- ICEROCKET blog search
- Google Blog Search BETA
- BlogPulse
- backtype

- serph
- Google trends
- Trendrr
- Google Insights for Search beta

Branding of an Individual

Create a website

See if you can register your name as the name of your website. In case it is not available, you could add your city's name or your pin code to the domain name; or your profession to the website name. Ensure you register the name that you are best known by.

After registering your domain name, create your website. If you don't want to spend too much on hosting fees, you could try Godaddy.com. It offers a free five page website and hosting with each domain name registered. You could create a simple site here explaining who you are, your hobbies and perhaps upload an updated resume.

Create a free blog

Use your name as the blog name and create a free blog on Wordpress.com or Blogger.com to take advantage of their credibility. With yourname.wordpress.com or yourname.blogger.com you will get another website to come up on a Google search for your name. You can share your thoughts online on your blog in a radically transparent manner.

Set up a social networking profile

Although you cannot manually set your URL on a social networking site, it will include your first name and last name. Besides building up your personal brand, it is another website to add to Google results for a search on your name. Here you can connect with customers, employers, investors, and media besides your friends, family and colleagues.

Share your photos

Flickr.com is a good place to share your photos with the world. You can use your name for the profile and customize the URL accordingly. Label your photos with your name and you will increase the chances of Google ranking the page.

Answer others' questions

Yahoo! Answers can help you rank well on Google too as you can take advantage of the fact that it is a sub domain of Yahoo. Although you cannot customize the URL here, you can select a profile name and include your name in the "About Me" section.

Social bookmarking profile

Even profiles on social bookmarking sites like digg.com, delicious.com and StumbleUpon.com are Google friendly. StumbleUpon allows you to use your real name in the profile and gives you a sub domain like yourname.stumbleupon.com.

Use shopping and review sites

Even if you don't buy anything on Amazon.com, you can still set up a profile there. This is likely to rank well on Google. As Google loves content, ensure you fill up your profile there. Set up your own shopping lists and product reviews.

Bring your profiles together

You could use Naymz.com to share links to all your social networking profiles. Profiles here generally rank well on Google.

Online
Reputation

Case Studies

5

Domino's

In 2009, two Domino's employees uploaded a video on YouTube as a prank. In the video, one employee prepared sandwiches by putting cheese up his nose, and then the spreading the nasal mucous on the sandwiches and the other employee commented simultaneously. In a few days, over 100,000 people had viewed it on YouTube. It came up frequently in the first page of Google search results for "Dominos" and discussions around it were happening on Twitter.

Domino's fired the two employees and charged them with felony. Domino's discarded all open containers of food at the concerned outlet, which cost them hundreds of dollars. The graphic video ensured that even decade old Domino's customers began to rethink their relationship with Domino's. Although the video was soon off YouTube, discussions in social media continued on what Domino's response would be.

The company realized they could not remain quiet. It created a Twitter account to address these comments and uploaded a video with its chief executive's take on the issue on YouTube. Relevant responses on the channels where discussions on this issue were happening helped Domino's come out relatively unscathed from this crisis.

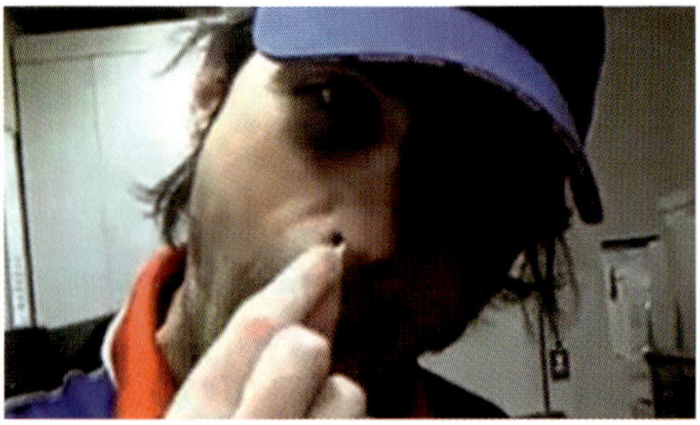

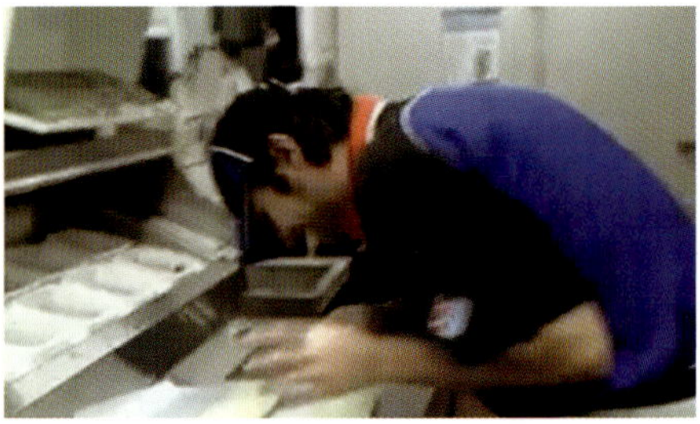

Nestle KitKat

Greenpeace launched a campaign against Nestle KitKat for obtaining palm oil from suppliers who it claimed were destroying the Indonesian rainforests, endangering the locals' livelihoods and were responsible for the near extinction of orangutans.

This campaign included a video posted by Greenpeace on YouTube showing a Nestle employee eating an orangutan finger in a KitKat pack. Nestlé's efforts to have the video removed simply resulted in a temporary change in the video's location.

Greenpeace then changed its Facebook UK page to a Nestle Killer mockup. It asked its supporters to share the video, change their profile picture to Nestle Killer and to boycott

Nestle products in protest. When Nestlé's Facebook page was overrun with negative comments and Nestle Killer profile pictures, a Nestle representative got into a verbal fight with fans. However, she apologized later.

Kodak

Eastman Kodak

Eastman Kodak launched "A Thousand Words" blog, authored by thousands of employees worldwide in 2006. The blog receives around 15000 to 20000 visitors every month. It engages employees and energizes them. The blog guidelines include using at least one photo per post, speedy response to comments, reaching out to friends, family and colleagues to increase the blog's viral marketing impact.

In one innovative post, an employee wondered what the world would look like from a dog's perspective. She attached her digital camera and Kodak's flexible legged Gorillapod tripod to her dog's collar. The results were several blurry pictures.

Apart from consumers, employees, professionals, Kodak blogs also reach journalists through press release RSS feeds and cross linking between blog posts and online releases on the Kodak corporate website. Company press releases often indicate that more information is available at a link to one of the blogs.

Kodak also produces two audio or video podcasts every month. "Kodak Close- Up" podcasts showcase company technology and strategy insights, supplemented by interviews with creative professionals and photographers. Podcasts are available on Kodak.com and the iTunes store. Many professionals enjoy the podcasts on their daily commutes.

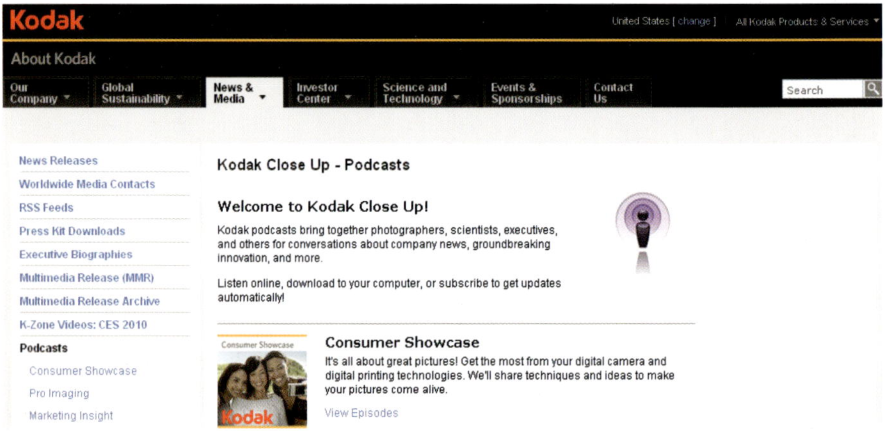

Barrack Obama

Obama's Organizing for America

Obama used social networking intensively for securing the Democratic nomination for the 2008 presidential election. He shared personal information like his love for basketball and Moby Dick on Facebook.

Obama also enabled his profile with many multimedia plug-in. More than 140,000 followers of his profile can browse over 300 photos; watch videos from his ralliesand interact with other campaign supporters. More than 15,000 comments have been left for Obama.

AquaFina

In the commodity bottled water market, AquaFina has succeeded in carving out a distinctive identity for itself, using social networking. It created its profile at myspace.com/aquafina to build brand loyalty before the consumer was in the outlet. Rather than merely using display advertising, Pepsi used this profile to create a community of users who were emotionally engaged with the brand.

It does so by running contests challenging users to create music videos or by hosting interactive games. AquaFina has 11,500 friends on MySpace and has attracted over 500 comments. The strong brand image created thereby helped cushion the negative impact of the news in 2007 that it was using purified tap water from a municipal water supply.

AquaFina has thus been able to reach out to its target demographic of 18-34 year olds through their preferred medium of social networking.

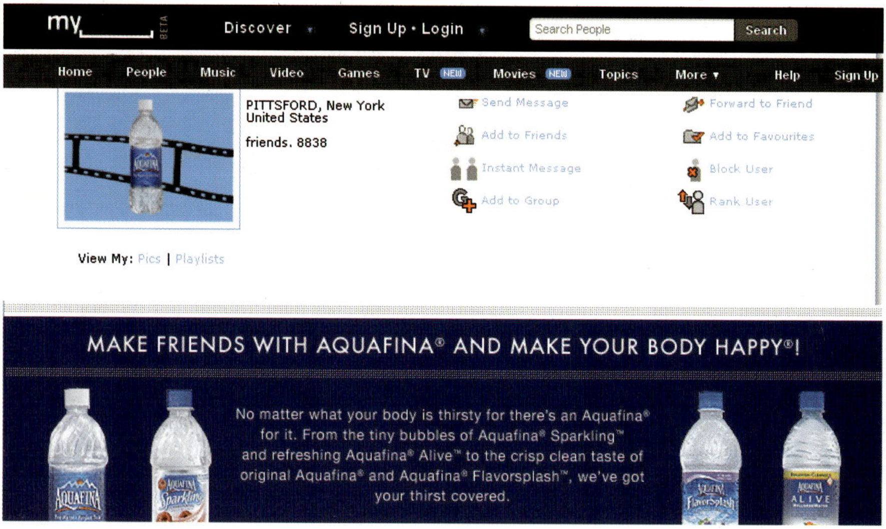

Lenovo

Lenovo closely tracks online mentions of its company name or it's most popular product line- ThinkPad. In 2006, Lenovo tracked a report about a laptop catching fire at Los Angeles International Airport. Other reports and photos identified it as a Lenovo ThinkPad. Lenovo's Vice President of Marketing learnt of this within four hours of the incident. He sent a team of Lenovo scientists to the Los Angeles International Airport within an hour to examine the laptop in question and record the incident. Meanwhile, the online conversation spread to other blogs and mainstream media. As Lenovo had identified the problem early on, it quickly discovered the fault was in a Sony supplied battery and issued recalls, as did Sony of the faulty batteries.

Lenovo India also monitors tweets for references to its name. It found one such tweet by a youth who was debating which laptop to buy. Lenovo sent him the specifications it was offering. The young man was so pleased with Lenovo's prompt response that he decided to buy a Lenovo.

Apple

When Apple CEO Steve Jobs announced the launch of the iPhone, one of the first images of the new device appeared on the photo sharing site Flickr. Almost immediately, the photo was submitted to the social voting site Digg.com by web designer Jeremy Flint. It soon gained enough votes to be deemed worthy of being displayed on the Digg.com home page.

In only a few hours, the photo had received thousands of votes. It finally got more than 24,000 "diggs" and hundreds of comments. This resulted in the photo getting over 150,000 page views and over 2000 web links and mentions by dozens of bloggers. Apple's iPhone launch was a big success on social media. Jeremy Flint earned a following of over 142 Digg users and acquired a reputation of being an Apple expert.

Nike

Athletic apparel maker Nike has built customized social communities. To attract fans from many sports, Nike has branded basketball (nikebasketball.com), football (nikefootball.com) and their biggest success (nike.com/nikeplus).

Nike Plus is a joint effort with Apple's iPod where runners can listen to music while they measure the calories they've burnt and the distance they've run. Members of this community can share songs and data with their friends, arrange running meetups and create exercise challenges. Besides helping Nike interact with its customers and build brand loyalty, Nike Plus is helping Nike win new customers.

Dell

Dell succeeded in establishing itself as a reputed, reliable laptop manufacturer from the late 90s. In the early 2000s, Dell decided to out source its technical support to India, to reduce costs. On June 21, 2005, influential blogger Jeff Jarvis coined the term "Dell Hell" on his blog. Jeff Jarvis is not a computer expert. When he bought his Dell notebook, he chose the four year, in home warranty service. He paid more for this service so that he would have peace of mind. However, Jarvis's Dell gave him a hard time. The hardware was problematic, he was unable to connect to the network, the CPU didn't work properly and the machine would keep overheating. When he tried to avail his warranty, he discovered that the technician visiting his home would not have the required parts. He would have to send his machine to Dell and therefore be without a computer for two weeks. Jarvis told this tale on his popular media and news blog BuzzMachine.com.

Others joined the conversation on his blog with their own stories of suffering due to Dell's diminishing customer support. Over the next three weeks, Jarvis published 12 posts on Dell's poor customer service. This attracted thousands of comments. Dell didn't know how to react, so it chose not to react at all. It issued no public statement on the crisis. Dell even closed its Dell Customer Support Forum.

People were unhappy with Dell's service before Jarvis's fateful blog post, but Jarvis served as a catalyst in this situation. Dell took nearly a year to decide being radically transparent was preferable to its policy of non engagement. Direct2dell.com was its first attempt at listening to what its customers had to say. A digital media manager was appointed to serve as a web community spokesperson on Dell products and service. Dell then launched blogs in multiple languages, created Studio Dell for podcasts and videos, increased the number of support forums to seven and even launched IdeaStorm.com- its own social networking community. Customers can suggest new products or services they would like to see Dell develop on IdeaStorm. More than 5000 ideas and 20000 comments came in the first three months of the launch of IdeaStorm.

Glossary

6

Blog An online journal that's updated on a regular basis with entries that appear in reverse chronological order. Blogs can be about any subject. They typically contain comments by other readers, links to other sites and permalinks.

Cloud computing Cloud computing (also called "the cloud") refers to the growing phenomenon of users who can access their data from anywhere rather than being tied to a particular machine.

Crowd sourcing Crowd sourcing refers to harnessing the skills and enthusiasm of those outside an organization who are prepared to volunteer their time contributing content or skills and solving problems.

Digital inclusion Digital inclusion, or e-inclusion, is an effort to help people who are not online gain access with affordable hardware, software, tech support/information and broadband Internet service, so they can begin to use this technology to improve their lives.

Digital story A digital story is a short personal nonfiction narrative that is composed on a computer, often for publishing online or publishing to a DVD. They are told from the narrator's point of view and the subject is generally about something the maker experienced personally. Digital Stories include music, art, photos, voice over and video clips. They are also typically created by one person with little technical training, rather than by a team of professionals.

Feed A Web feed or RSS feed is a format that provides users with frequently updated content. Content distributors syndicate a Web feed, enabling users to subscribe to a site's latest content. By using a news reader to subscribe to a feed, you can read the latest posts or watch the newest videos on your computer or portable device on your own schedule.

Flash mob

A flash mob is a group of individuals who gather and disperse with little notice for a specific purpose through text messages, Social Media or viral e-mails.

GPS

GPS or Global Positioning System, a global navigation satellite system. GPS-enabled devices - most commonly mobile handhelds or a car's navigation system - enable precise pinpointing of the location of people, buildings and objects.

Hosting

A blog, video or podcast needs a hosting service before it can appear online. Companies sometimes host their blogs on their own servers, but a better choice for video or audio is to use a host such as YouTube, Viddler or Magnify.net for video and a host such as Libsyn for podcasts.

İnternet newsroom

An İnternet newsroom also called İnternet pressroom or online media center is an area of a corporate website that communicates corporate messages and makes content available to the news media and the public. A true İnternet newsroom incorporates features such as videos, podcasts, high-resolution image galleries, surveys, forums, blogs and other online marketing communications materials.

Mashup

Mashups (or mash-ups) have several meanings. A music mashup is a combination of two or more songs, generally the vocals of one song overlaid on top of the melody of another. A video mashup is the result of combining two or more pieces of video, such as news footage with original commentary. A Web mashup results when a programmer overlays information from a database or another source on top of an existing website, such as homes for sale taken from Craigslist plotted on a Google Map.

Metadata Information-including titles, descriptions, tags and captions- that describes a media item such as a video, photo or blog post. Some kinds of metadata-e.g., camera settings such as exposure, aperture, focal length and ISO speed - can be captured automatically from the device without needing a human to enter the data.

Microblogging The act of broadcasting short messages to other subscribers of a Web service. On Twitter, entries are limited to 140 characters, and applications like Plurk and Jaiku take a similar approach with sharing bite-size media.

Moblog A blog published directly to the Web from a phone or other mobile device. Mobloggers may update their sites more frequently than other bloggers because they don't need to be at their computers to post.

Open source In its strict sense, open source refers to a software code that is free to build upon. But it has taken on a broader meaning - such as open source journalism and open source politics - to refer to the practice of collaboration and free sharing of media and information to advance the public good. Well-known open-source projects include the Linux operating system, the Apache Web server and the Firefox browser.

RSS RSS (Really Simple Syndication) - sometimes called web feeds - is a Web standard for the delivery of content - blog entries, news stories, headlines, images, and video - enabling readers to stay current with favourite publications or producers without having to browse from site to site. All blogs, podcasts and videoblogs contain an RSS feed, which lets users subscribe to content automatically and read or listen to the material on a computer or a portable device.

Screencast A screencast is a video that captures what takes place on a computer screen, usually accompanied by audio narration. It is often created to explain how a website or piece of software works, but it can be any piece of explanatory video that strings together images or visual elements.

Search engine marketing Search engine marketing (SEM) is a series of online tactics that, when combined with SEO, helps to attract customers, generate brand awareness and build trust. SEM (sometimes called search marketing) seeks to increase websites' visibility chiefly through the purchase of pay-per-click ads and paid inclusion.

Search engine optimization Search engine optimization (SEO) is the process of arranging your website to give it the best chance of appearing near the top of search engine rankings. As an Internet marketing strategy, SEO considers how search engines work and what people search for. Optimizing a website primarily involves editing its content, identifying high-traffic keywords and improving the site's layout and design.

Smart phone A handheld device capable of advanced tasks beyond those of a standard mobile phone. Capabilities might include email, chat, taking photos or video or hundreds of other tasks.

Social bookmarking Social bookmarking is a method by which users locate, store, organize, share and manage bookmarks of Web pages without being tied to a particular machine. Users store lists of personally interesting Internet resources and usually make these lists publicly accessible. Delicious is the best-known social bookmark site.

Social capital

Social capital is a concept used in business, nonprofits and other arenas that refers to the goodwill and positive reputation that flows to a person through his or her relationships with others in social networks.

Social Media optimization

Social Media Optimization (SMO) is a set of practices for generating publicity through Social Media, online communities and social networks. The focus is on driving traffic from sources other than search engines, though improved search ranking is also a benefit of successful SMO.

Streaming media

A video or audio that can be watched or listened to online but not stored permanently. Streamed audio is often called Webcasting. Traditional media companies like to stream their programs so that they can't be distributed freely onto file-sharing networks.

Tags

Keywords added to a blog post, photo or video to help users find related topics or media, either through browsing on the site or as a term to make your entry more relevant to search engines.

Tweet

A post on Twitter, a real-time social messaging system. While all agree on usage of tweet as a noun, people disagree on whether you "tweet" or "twitter" as a verb. RT stands for retweet: Users add RT in a tweet if they are reposting something from another person's tweet.

UGC

UGC stands for user-generated content, an industry term that refers to all forms of user-created materials such as blog posts, reviews, podcasts, videos, comments and more.

Web analytics

Web analytics is the measurement, collection, analysis and reporting of Internet data for the purpose of understanding who your visitors are and optimizing your website.

Web conferencing

Web conferencing is used to conduct live meetings or presentations over the Internet. In a web conference, each participant sits at his or her own computer and is connected to other participants via the Internet. This can be either a downloaded application on each of the attendees' computers or a web-based application where the attendees enter a URL (website address) to enter the conference.

Webcasting

The ability to use the Web to deliver live or delayed versions of audio or video broadcasts. Listeners can tune into webcasts from anywhere in the world,and can also receive textual or visual data (artist and song titles, ads, album artwork, etc.) during a webcast.

Webinar

Short for Web-based seminar, a webinar is a presentation, lecture, workshop or seminar that is transmitted over the Web. In general, participants register in advance and access the presentation in real time over the Internet and listen to the presenter either through computer speakers or a telephone connection. Webinars are generally one-way and can involve chat or polls.

Widget

A widget, sometimes called a gadget, badge or applet, is a small block of content, typically displayed in a small box, with a specific purpose, such as providing weather forecasts or news, that is constantly updating itself (typically via RSS). Widgets make it easy to add dynamic content to your site or blog.

Wiki

A collaborative website that can be directly edited by anyone with access to it. Small teams often find that they can accomplish a task more easily by creating a collaborative online workspace using wiki software such as pbworks, Socialtext or mediawiki.

Wikipedia

A web-based, multi-language, free-content encyclopedia written collaboratively by volunteers. Sponsored by the non-profit Wikimedia Foundation, it has editions in about 200 different languages.

Word-of-mouth marketing

Word-of-mouth marketing, sometimes called grassroots marketing or conversational marketing, is an umbrella term for dozens of techniques that can be used to engage and energize customers.

Conclusion

Online reputation management may be in its infancy. However, if you plan now to control your reputation in the digital space, you will reap the benefits for years to come. Now you know that you should maintain a transparent voice online, throughout your communication. Trust your consumers in turn to provide honest and relevant feedback about your brands and your company. Just as a reputation is built by how others perceive you, it is often what others say about you online that influences your online reputation. By engaging in constant dialogue and providing value adding content to all your stakeholders, you can ensure that you are the first company your consumers and potential consumers consider when purchasing products in your line of business.

Bibliography

Some of the information in the book has been compiled from the vast resources available online and after referring multiple books. The information has also been presented in accordance with our own experiences. We acknowledge and thank all the sources on the World Wide Web which have contributed in completing this book. This book is meant to provide information only, and is not to be used as a guide for advice or suggestions. A professional must be consulted for the same.

Suggested Reading

- **Dentsu Social Media Handbook**, Popular Prakashan, 2010

- Andy Beal and Dr. Judy Strauss, **Radically Transparent, Monitoring and managing reputations online**, Wiley Publishing, Inc., Indianapolis, Indiana, 2008

- Brogan, Chris, and Julien Smith, **Trust Agents: Using the Web to Build Influence, Improve Reputation, and Earn Trust.** Hoboken, NJ: John Wiley & Sons, 2009

AIRCEL
Your voice has made a difference.
A Big Thank You.
SAVE OUR TIGERS
An Aircel Initiative